AI SIMPLIFIED

A Beginner's Guide to Understanding Artificial Intelligence

David Sullivan

TABLE OF CONTENTS

CHAPTER 1

INTRODUCTION TO ARTIFICIAL INTELLIGENCE

Welcome to the world of Artificial Intelligence (AI), a fascinating and rapidly evolving field that has become an integral part of our modern lives. AI is at the heart of numerous technologies and applications that we encounter every day, from voice assistants like Siri and Google Assistant to personalized movie recommendations on streaming platforms like Netflix. It powers the algorithms that shape social media feeds and enables self-driving cars to navigate our roads safely.

But what exactly is AI? How does it work, and why is it so important in today's world? This introductory guide aims to provide you with the answers to these questions and more. Whether you're a curious individual with little to no background in AI or a professional exploring the potential of this transformative technology, this handbook will demystify the complexities and jargon surrounding AI, making it accessible to everyone.

What is Artificial Intelligence?

Artificial Intelligence (AI) is a term used to describe the development of computer systems that can perform tasks that typically require human intelligence. It involves creating machines that can think, learn, and make decisions like humans, but using data and algorithms instead of human reasoning.

At its core, AI aims to replicate human cognitive abilities such as problem-solving, pattern recognition, speech and language understanding, and decision-making. This technology allows computers to process vast amounts of data, identify patterns within it, and draw conclusions or predictions from that information.

AI comes in various forms, such as machine learning, which enables systems to learn from data and improve their performance over time. Deep learning, a subset of machine learning, involves artificial neural networks that mimic the human brain's structure and functioning. These neural networks process data through layers, enabling them to recognize complex patterns and features in the data.

You encounter AI in your daily life more than you might realize. Smart assistants like Siri, Google Assistant, and Alexa use AI to understand and respond to your voice commands. Social media platforms employ AI algorithms to personalize your news feed and show content that matches your interests. Online shopping websites use AI to recommend products based on your past purchases and browsing behavior.

AI also plays a vital role in industries like healthcare, where it aids in medical diagnostics, drug development, and personalized treatment plans. In the automotive sector, AI powers self-driving cars to navigate and make decisions on the road. Additionally, AI is utilized in finance for fraud detection, in agriculture for crop optimization, and in entertainment for creating lifelike characters in video games.

While AI offers numerous benefits, there are also concerns about its ethical implications and potential biases in decision-making. Striking the right balance between technological advancement and ethical considerations is a critical challenge that needs to be addressed as AI continues to evolve.

Brief History of AI

The history of artificial intelligence (AI) dates back to ancient times, where myths and legends depicted the creation of intelligent, lifelike beings. However, the modern development of AI began in the mid-20th century with the advent of computers and the theoretical groundwork laid by pioneering researchers.

In the 1940s, during World War II, the first electronic computers were built to assist in military calculations. It was during this time that the concept of "universal machines" was introduced by mathematician and logician Alan Turing. Turing's work laid the foundation for the notion of machines that could simulate any human intelligence.

In the 1950s, the term "artificial intelligence" was coined, and the field of AI officially began to take shape. A significant moment in this decade was the development of the first AI program, known as the Logic Theorist, by Allen Newell and Herbert A. Simon. It could prove mathematical theorems using a formalized logic system.

During the 1960s and 1970s, AI research saw remarkable progress. The development of the General Problem Solver (GPS) by Newell and Simon demonstrated the potential of AI to tackle a wide range of problems. In 1966, the first AI laboratory, the Stanford Artificial Intelligence Laboratory (SAIL), was established, fostering further research and collaboration in the field.

However, the early successes of AI research were followed by a period known as the "AI winter" in the 1970s and 1980s. High expectations and limited computing power led to disappointment, causing a decline in AI funding and research. Nevertheless, during this time, expert systems emerged as a popular AI application, employing rule-based systems to mimic human decision-making.

In the late 1980s and 1990s, the AI field experienced a resurgence. Advances in computing power and the development of new algorithms, such as neural networks, reignited interest in AI research. The field of machine learning began to flourish, enabling AI systems to learn from data and improve their performance over time.

The early 21st century marked significant milestones for AI. In 2011, IBM's Watson defeated human champions in the quiz show "Jeopardy!", demonstrating how AI can effectively manage natural language processing and vast volumes of data. Around the same time, breakthroughs in deep learning, a subset of machine learning, revolutionized the field by enabling AI models to process complex data and make sophisticated decisions.

In recent years, AI has become an integral part of various industries and applications. AI-powered technologies, including virtual assistants, recommendation systems, and autonomous vehicles, have become increasingly prevalent in our daily lives. The ongoing advancements in AI are driving innovations in fields such as healthcare, finance, transportation, and more.

Why AI Matters in Today's World

In the 21st century, AI has become an integral part of our modern society, driving innovation and transforming various industries. From virtual assistants like Siri, Google Assistant, and Alexa that respond to our voice commands to personalized content recommendations on streaming platforms like

Netflix and Spotify, AI has made our daily tasks more efficient and convenient.

AI is at the heart of technologies that power social media platforms, enabling personalized news feeds and content curation. It also plays a crucial role in the development of self-driving cars, promising safer and more efficient transportation systems.

In the healthcare sector, AI applications are revolutionizing medical diagnostics, drug discovery, and treatment plans, leading to improved patient outcomes and better disease management.

Financial institutions leverage AI algorithms to optimize trading strategies, detect fraudulent activities, and enhance customer service, contributing to a more robust and secure financial ecosystem.

In education, AI-powered adaptive learning platforms cater to individual student needs, offering personalized learning experiences that improve overall academic performance and engagement.

Moreover, AI's potential extends to environmental sustainability, where it is utilized to analyze and manage vast amounts of environmental data, facilitating better conservation efforts and promoting a greener future.

Ethical Considerations in AI Development

While AI offers immense potential, it also presents ethical challenges that require careful consideration and responsible development. As AI systems make decisions and predictions that impact individuals and societies, ethical concerns such as bias, fairness, transparency, and accountability become paramount.

Biases in AI algorithms can arise from biased training data, leading to unfair treatment of certain groups or reinforcing societal prejudices. Ensuring fairness and mitigating bias in AI systems is an ongoing area of research and ethical focus.

Data privacy is another critical aspect. AI relies heavily on data, and safeguarding user information is essential to maintain trust and prevent potential misuse.

Transparency in AI decision-making is vital to understand how AI arrives at its conclusions, especially in critical applications like healthcare and legal decision support systems.

As AI technologies continue to advance, ensuring that developers, researchers, and policymakers adhere to ethical guidelines becomes a collective responsibility.

Throughout this handbook, we will delve into these ethical considerations, guiding you through the best practices and responsible AI development principles that can pave the way for a more equitable and ethical AI-powered future.

CHAPTER 2

UNDERSTANDING THE BASICS Of

AI

Artificial Intelligence has become a ubiquitous term in our modern world, and its impact is felt in various aspects of our daily lives, from personalized recommendations on entertainment platforms to voice-activated smart assistants that answer our questions with remarkable accuracy. However, the world of AI can often seem complex and overwhelming, filled with technical jargon and intricate algorithms that may appear beyond our grasp.

Fear not, as our aim in this chapter is to simplify these concepts and present them in a way that anyone can understand. Whether you're a curious individual with no prior knowledge of AI or a tech enthusiast looking to deepen your understanding, this chapter will serve as your stepping stone into the captivating realm of AI.

Machine Learning vs. Deep Learning vs. Neural Networks

Machine Learning

Machine Learning (ML) is a subset of artificial intelligence that focuses on building computer programs capable of learning and improving from experience without being explicitly programmed. In traditional programming, we provide specific instructions to solve a problem, but in machine learning, we give the computer data and allow it to learn patterns and relationships within the data to make decisions or predictions.

In general, machine learning usually comprises these stages:

1. Data Collection: Gathering relevant data from various sources. This data becomes the foundation for training the machine learning model.

2. Data Preprocessing: Cleaning and organizing the data to remove errors, inconsistencies, and irrelevant information. Preprocessing ensures that the data is in a suitable format for the machine learning algorithm.

3. Feature Extraction: Identifying the important features or patterns within the data that will help the machine learning model make accurate predictions.

4. Model Training: Using the preprocessed data, the machine learning model is trained on a

specific algorithm to learn patterns and relationships in the data.

5. Model Evaluation: The trained model is tested on a separate dataset to measure its accuracy and performance.

6. Model Deployment: If the model performs well, it can be deployed in real-world applications to make predictions or automate decision-making processes.

Machine learning is used in various applications, such as email filtering (spam vs. non-spam classification), recommendation systems (e.g., Netflix movie recommendations), fraud detection, medical diagnosis, and many more.

Deep Learning

Deep Learning is a subfield of machine learning that focuses on using artificial neural networks to model and solve complex problems. These neural networks are inspired by the structure and functioning of the human brain, consisting of layers of interconnected nodes called neurons.

The key feature of deep learning is the ability to automatically learn hierarchical representations of data. Unlike traditional machine learning, which requires human-engineered feature extraction, deep learning models can learn abstract features from raw data, making them highly adaptable and powerful..

Neural Networks

Neural Networks are the fundamental building blocks of deep learning. They are a collection of interconnected nodes organized in layers. Each node, or neuron, takes input data, performs a simple computation, and passes the output to the next layer. This process continues through multiple layers until the final output is produced.

The structure of a neural network is typically organized into three types of layers:

1. Input Layer: The first layer that receives the raw data as input.
2. Hidden Layers: Layers between the input and output layers where most of the computation and feature extraction occur.
3. Output Layer: The output layer is the last layer responsible for generating the model's predictions or results.
4. The strength of neural networks lies in their ability to automatically learn complex patterns and representations from vast amounts of data. For example, in image recognition tasks, a deep

learning model can learn to recognize objects, faces, or even intricate patterns from raw pixel values without human intervention.

Deep learning has seen significant success in tasks like image and speech recognition, natural language processing, playing games (e.g., AlphaGo), autonomous vehicles, and much more.

Supervised, Unsupervised, and Reinforcement Learning

Supervised Learning

Supervised learning is a type of machine learning where the algorithm learns from labeled training data to make predictions or classifications. In this approach, the dataset provided to the algorithm contains input-output pairs, where the input is the data (features), and the output is the corresponding target or label.

For instance, consider a simple task of predicting whether an email is spam or not. The algorithm is provided with a large set of emails, each labeled as "spam" or "not spam." The algorithm learns from these examples and generalizes the patterns in the data to classify new, unseen emails as either spam or not spam.

The key steps in supervised learning are:

- o Data Collection: Gathering labeled data to build the training dataset.
- o Data Preprocessing: tidying up and organizing the data before it can be used for training.
- o Model Selection: Choosing an appropriate algorithm or model for the task.

- Model Training: Using the labeled data to adjust the model's parameters and optimize its performance.
- Model Evaluation: Assessing the model's accuracy and effectiveness using a separate test dataset.

Some common examples of supervised learning tasks include image classification, language translation, sentiment analysis, and regression tasks like predicting house prices based on features like area, location, etc.

Unsupervised Learning

Unsupervised learning, as the name suggests, does not involve labeled data. Instead, the algorithm tries to find patterns and relationships within the data without any specific guidance. In unsupervised learning, the dataset contains only the input data (features) without corresponding output labels.

A classic example of unsupervised learning is clustering. Imagine a dataset of customer purchase behavior in a supermarket. The algorithm will group customers with similar purchase habits into clusters without knowing any predefined categories. This process helps identify customer segments for targeted marketing strategies.

Key steps in unsupervised learning include:

- Data Collection: Gathering the raw data without labeled outputs.
- Data Preprocessing: Tidying up and organizing the data before it can be used for training.

- Model Selection: Choosing an appropriate algorithm for clustering or dimensionality reduction.
- Model Training: Running the algorithm to identify patterns and relationships in the data.
- Post-Processing: Analyzing the results and interpreting the clusters or patterns.

Other unsupervised learning tasks include anomaly detection, data compression, and feature extraction for dimensionality reduction.

Reinforcement Learning

Reinforcement learning is a different approach to machine learning, where an agent learns to interact with an environment to achieve specific goals. The agent engages in actions within its surroundings and gains responses through rewards or punishments. The objective of the agent is to optimize the total rewards it accumulates throughout its interactions. Imagine teaching an AI to play a game. The AI agent will take actions (moves) in the game, and based on its performance, it will receive rewards or penalties. Over time, it learns the best sequence of actions to achieve the highest rewards (winning the game).

Key components of reinforcement learning are:

- Agent: The AI algorithm that takes actions in the environment.
- Environment: The external realm in which the agent engages.
- Action: The set of possible moves or decisions the agent can make.

- Reward: The feedback given to the agent after each action.
- Policy: The strategy or set of rules guiding the agent's decision-making process.

Reinforcement learning is used in scenarios like game playing, autonomous vehicles, robotics, and optimizing business processes.

CHAPTER 3

AI IN DAY-TO-DAY ACTIVITIES

AI has become an integral part of our everyday lives, simplifying tasks and enhancing convenience in numerous ways. From smart assistants like Siri, Google Assistant, and Alexa that respond to our voice commands and assist with various tasks, to personalized recommendations on platforms like Netflix and Spotify, AI is all around us. Social media platforms like Facebook and Twitter also utilize AI algorithms to curate our feeds and suggest content tailored to our interests. Additionally, AI plays a crucial role in virtual shopping experiences, optimizing product recommendations and improving customer satisfaction. Furthermore, in the healthcare sector, AI aids in medical diagnostics and research, enabling faster and more accurate outcomes. This chapter in "AI Simplified: Your Beginner's Handbook to Artificial Intelligence" explores how AI is seamlessly integrated into our daily routines, making life more efficient and enjoyable.

AI in Smart Assistants

Smart Assistants, such as Siri (Apple), Google Assistant (Google), and Alexa (Amazon), are revolutionary AI-powered applications designed to assist users with various tasks and provide convenient hands-free interaction with devices. These smart assistants leverage advanced natural language processing (NLP), machine learning, and voice recognition technologies to understand and respond to user commands and queries.

The heart of these smart assistants is their AI-driven NLP algorithms, which enable them to comprehend human language, context, and intent. They can interpret spoken language or written text, allowing users to engage in natural conversations with their devices. This capability enables smart assistants to perform a wide range of tasks, such as setting reminders, sending messages, making calls, providing weather updates, searching the web, and even controlling smart home devices.

Using Smart Assistants

If you're new to using smart assistants and AI-powered devices, getting started is remarkably straightforward. To use a smart assistant, you need a compatible device with an internet connection. This could be a smartphone, tablet, smart speaker, or even a smartwatch. Let's take a look at the basic steps to start using a smart assistant:

- Setting Up Your Device: Begin by turning on your device and connecting it to the internet.

For most modern smartphones and smart speakers, the initial setup process will guide you through connecting to Wi-Fi and signing in with your Google, Apple, or Amazon account.

- Activating the Smart Assistant: Each smart assistant has its own unique wake word or activation phrase. For example, saying "Hey Siri" activates Siri on Apple devices, "Okay Google" activates Google Assistant, and "Alexa" wakes up the Amazon Echo with Alexa onboard. Simply say the wake word, and the smart assistant will be ready to listen to your commands.

- Issuing Voice Commands: Once the smart assistant is activated and listening, you can start issuing voice commands or asking questions. For instance, you could say, "Set a reminder for

3 PM." The smart assistant will analyze your command, process it using AI algorithms, and provide a relevant response or perform the requested action.

- Interacting Naturally: One of the remarkable features of smart assistants is their ability to understand context and follow-up questions. You can have natural conversations, asking follow-up questions without repeating the context. As an illustration, you could inquire about the victor of the game from the previous evening and subsequently inquire about the timing of the upcoming match without indicating the specific team involved.

- Exploring Available Skills: Smart assistants have additional capabilities known as skills or actions, which allow them to integrate with third-party services and perform a more extensive range of tasks. For instance, you can enable skills to order food, play games, check flight status, control smart home devices, and much more.

- Privacy and Security Considerations: Remember that smart assistants are always listening for their wake words to activate, which raises privacy concerns for some users. It's essential to review and adjust the privacy settings on your devices according to your preferences.

AI in Personalized Recommendations (e.g., Netflix, Spotify)

One of the most prominent and beneficial applications of artificial intelligence is in personalized recommendations. Services like Netflix and Spotify utilize AI algorithms to analyze user behavior, preferences, and historical data to provide tailored content and music suggestions. These platforms collect vast amounts of data on what users watch or listen to, how long they engage with certain content, and what they have liked or disliked in the past. AI algorithms then process this data to create personalized recommendations, enhancing the user experience and keeping users engaged with their platforms.

For instance, on Netflix, the recommendation system uses collaborative filtering and content-based filtering algorithms. Collaborative filtering analyzes patterns in user behavior and identifies users with similar tastes, making suggestions based on what other like-minded users have enjoyed. On the other hand, content-based filtering looks at the attributes of the content itself and recommends similar items based on specific features.

By combining these approaches, Netflix creates a powerful recommendation engine that can introduce users to new movies and TV shows they are likely to enjoy.

Similarly, Spotify employs AI algorithms to deliver personalized music recommendations. The platform examines user listening history, playlists, and interactions with songs to build a comprehensive profile of each user's musical taste. Using this data, Spotify's AI-powered recommendation system suggests new songs, artists, and playlists that align with the user's preferences, helping them discover new music effortlessly.

How to Use AI Personalized Recommendations
If you're a beginner looking to make the most out of AI-powered personalized recommendations, here's a simple guide to get started:

- Create an Account: Sign up for an account on the platform of your choice, such as Netflix or Spotify. This will allow the AI system to start collecting data on your interactions and preferences.

- Start Interacting: Begin using the platform to watch movies or listen to music. The more you engage with content, the more data the AI system will have to work with, leading to better recommendations over time.

- Rate and Review: Many platforms allow you to rate or review the content you've consumed. Take advantage of this feature by providing feedback on the movies you've watched or the songs you've listened to. This will help the AI system understand your preferences better.

- Explore Recommendations: Once you've been using the platform for a while, explore the personalized recommendation sections. On Netflix, you'll find recommendations based on your viewing history and similar users. On Spotify, you'll find playlists and music suggestions tailored to your tastes.

- Discover New Content: Don't be afraid to try out the recommended content. AI algorithms are designed to introduce you to new things you might like. If you enjoy the recommendations, the AI system will learn even more about your preferences.

- Fine-Tune Preferences: If you receive recommendations that don't resonate with you, you can always fine-tune your preferences.

Some platforms allow you to give explicit feedback, such as thumbs up or thumbs down, on individual recommendations, helping the AI system learn from your choices.

- Engage Regularly: To keep the AI system up-to-date with your evolving tastes, continue using the platform regularly and exploring new content. The more data the AI system has, the better it can tailor recommendations to your preferences.

AI in Social Media

AI has become an integral part of the social media landscape, powering many features and functionalities that users interact with daily on platforms like Facebook, Twitter, Instagram, and more. The implementation of AI in social media has transformed the way we connect, share, and engage with content.

By analyzing vast amounts of user data and patterns, AI algorithms can deliver personalized experiences, relevant content, and targeted advertisements. Let's explore how AI enhances various aspects of social media platforms and how to use it as a beginner, step by step.

- Personalized Content and Recommendations: AI algorithms in social media analyze user behavior, preferences, and interactions to deliver personalized content to users. For instance, your Facebook newsfeed shows posts based on your interests, engagement history, and connections. Similarly, Twitter uses AI to recommend relevant tweets and accounts to follow based on your activity. As a beginner, you can experience this AI-driven personalization by engaging with posts, liking content, and following users that interest you.

The more you interact, the more the AI system learns about your preferences, leading to more tailored content.

- Automated Moderation and Content Filtering: AI plays a crucial role in moderating content and maintaining a safe social media environment. It can automatically detect and remove inappropriate or offensive posts, spam, and fake accounts. Social media platforms employ AI models to identify hate speech, abusive content, and misinformation. As a user, you can benefit from this by reporting inappropriate content, which helps improve the AI's ability to detect and filter harmful material.

- Image and Video Recognition: AI-driven image and video recognition are used to enhance user experience on social media platforms. For example, Facebook can automatically tag your friends in photos using facial recognition AI algorithms. Additionally, AI helps identify and remove copyrighted content or sensitive material from being shared without permission. As a user, you can experience this by uploading images and videos, and AI will assist in recognizing faces, objects, and potential copyright issues.

- Sentiment Analysis and Feedback:Social media platforms utilize AI for sentiment analysis, which gauges the emotions and reactions of users to specific content or events. This analysis helps companies understand user feedback and improve their services. As a beginner, you can contribute to this by expressing your reactions through likes, comments, and shares, which allows AI to assess the sentiment around different posts and topics.

- Ad Targeting and Personalized Ads: AI-powered algorithms enable targeted advertising on social media. Advertisers can leverage user data to create personalized ad campaigns tailored to specific demographics, interests, and behaviors. As a user, you'll experience this through seeing ads that are more relevant to your preferences. Interacting with ads (e.g., clicking on them or providing feedback) helps AI fine-tune the targeting and offer more accurate advertisements.

- AI Chatbots for Customer Support: AI chatbots are increasingly used for customer support on social media platforms. These chatbots can quickly respond to common queries, provide assistance, and even handle basic transactions. As a user, you might encounter chatbots when seeking help or engaging with businesses through direct messages.

Using AI in social media as a beginner is as simple as interacting with the platform regularly. By engaging with content, following accounts that interest you, and expressing your preferences, you contribute to the AI's learning process and receive more personalized experiences. It's essential to be aware of your privacy settings and review how much data you're willing to share with social media platforms. By doing so, you can enjoy the benefits of AI-driven social media while maintaining control over your online presence. As AI continues to advance, social media platforms will undoubtedly introduce more innovative features, making the user experience even more personalized and engaging.

AI in Virtual Shopping and E-commerce

AI has revolutionized the way we shop online, providing personalized and immersive experiences for consumers. In virtual shopping and e-commerce, AI is used to enhance various aspects of the shopping journey, from product discovery and recommendations to customer support and post-purchase services. By leveraging advanced algorithms and data analytics, AI enables online retailers to understand customer preferences, predict behavior, and optimize the overall shopping experience.

One of the key applications of AI in virtual shopping is personalized product recommendations. AI algorithms analyze a customer's browsing and purchase history, as well as the behavior of similar users, to suggest products that match their preferences. This enables e-commerce platforms to present relevant and enticing product options, increasing the chances of converting a visitor into a customer.

For newbies looking to make the most out of virtual shopping with AI, it's as simple as using an online store and allowing the AI to work its magic. As you browse and interact with products, the AI system will start to learn about your interests and preferences. It will then recommend products tailored to your tastes, helping you discover items that align with your style and needs. For example, if you're shopping for clothing, the AI might suggest outfits based on your previous purchases, the current fashion trends, and the preferences of users with similar tastes.

Furthermore, AI is increasingly being used to enhance the virtual shopping experience through visual technologies. Virtual reality (VR) and augmented reality (AR) have become more prevalent in e-commerce, allowing customers to virtually try on products like clothing, accessories, or even furniture. AI algorithms help in mapping and tracking customer movements, ensuring a seamless and interactive experience. For instance, using a VR headset, you can "try on" various pairs of sunglasses, and the AI will simulate how each pair looks on your face in real-time.

Moreover, AI-powered chatbots and virtual assistants are becoming increasingly popular in e-commerce. These bots provide immediate and personalized customer support, guiding users through their shopping journey and answering questions about products, shipping, or returns. AI chatbots can handle multiple customer interactions simultaneously, reducing response times and improving overall customer satisfaction.

For newbies who want to make the most of AI-powered virtual shopping, simply engage with the chatbot or virtual assistant on the e-commerce website or app. These AI-driven helpers will be ready to assist you with any queries you might have, offer product recommendations, and ensure a smooth shopping experience.

AI in Healthcare and Medical Diagnostics

Artificial Intelligence has made significant strides in revolutionizing the healthcare industry, particularly in medical diagnostics. By leveraging machine learning algorithms and deep learning techniques, AI systems can analyze vast amounts of medical data and make accurate predictions and diagnoses. The applications of AI in healthcare range from improving disease detection to assisting in treatment decisions, ultimately leading to better patient outcomes and more efficient healthcare delivery.

One of the primary areas where AI has shown great promise is medical imaging. Traditional medical imaging techniques like X-rays, MRIs, and CT scans generate vast volumes of data that can be time-consuming for human radiologists to interpret. AI algorithms, however, can quickly analyze these images, identifying abnormalities, and assisting in the early detection of diseases like cancer, fractures, or cardiovascular issues. With AI's assistance, medical professionals can streamline their diagnostic process, reducing the time required for diagnosis and potentially catching critical conditions at earlier, more treatable stages.

Artificial intelligence also holds a vital position in the realm of personalized medicine. By analyzing a patient's genetic data, lifestyle factors, and medical history, AI algorithms can predict an individual's risk of developing certain diseases or responding to specific treatments. This enables healthcare providers to tailor treatment plans to each patient's unique needs, improving treatment efficacy and minimizing adverse effects. For instance, AI can help determine the most appropriate medications and dosages for patients based on their genetic makeup, enhancing the overall quality of healthcare.

Furthermore, AI-powered chatbots and virtual health assistants are becoming increasingly popular tools in the healthcare sector. These systems can interact with patients, gathering information about their symptoms and medical history, and provide preliminary diagnoses or recommend suitable medical care. While these virtual assistants are not meant to replace human doctors, they can act as valuable tools for triage and patient engagement, ensuring that patients receive timely medical attention and support.

If you are new to the concept of AI in healthcare and medical diagnostics, understanding its implementation can be simplified through the following steps:

- Familiarize Yourself with AI Basics: Start by grasping the fundamental concepts of artificial intelligence, such as machine learning, deep learning, and neural networks. These building blocks will help you understand how AI algorithms process and analyze medical data.

- Explore AI Applications in Healthcare: Discover the various ways AI is being used in the medical field, including medical imaging, personalized medicine, and virtual health assistants. Understanding these real-world use cases will give you insight into the practical impact of AI on patient care.

- Learn About AI Data Collection and Preprocessing: AI algorithms require large datasets to learn from. Learn how medical data is collected, anonymized, and prepared for AI analysis while ensuring patient privacy and data security.

- Get to Know AI Tools and Platforms: Explore user-friendly AI platforms designed for healthcare applications. These platforms often come with pre-built AI models that can be used for medical image analysis and predictive diagnostics, making it easier for beginners to implement AI solutions.

- Collaborate with Healthcare Professionals: Engage with healthcare practitioners and data scientists to gain a comprehensive understanding of the challenges and benefits of AI in medical diagnostics. Collaborating with experts can provide valuable insights and ensure responsible AI deployment.

- Embrace AI Ethical Considerations: As with any AI application, healthcare AI must be developed and used responsibly. Learn about the ethical considerations, potential biases, and fairness issues that may arise in healthcare AI to ensure patient safety and trust in the technology.

CHAPTER 4

GETTING STARTED With AI

Getting started with AI involves a series of essential steps to build a foundational understanding of the technology and begin exploring its applications. Firstly, familiarize yourself with the basic concepts of AI, such as machine learning and neural networks. Online courses, tutorials, and books tailored for beginners can provide a gentle introduction. Next, select a programming language like Python, which is widely used in AI development, and grasp the fundamentals of coding. Several online platforms offer interactive coding exercises and AI-specific libraries that facilitate experimentation.

Once you have a grasp of the basics, start small by creating your first AI model. Choose a simple project like image recognition or sentiment analysis to apply what you've learned. Begin with pre-built AI models available in popular libraries like TensorFlow or PyTorch, and gradually progress to customizing and training your models using relevant datasets. Continuously seek learning opportunities, stay updated on AI advancements, and participate in AI communities to share knowledge and gain insights from others on your journey into the exciting world of artificial intelligence.

Setting Up Your AI Development Environment

Setting up your AI development environment may sound intimidating, but fear not! We'll walk you through the process step-by-step, making it easy for beginners to get started with artificial intelligence. A well-configured AI development environment is crucial for efficiently building and experimenting with AI models. Let's dive in and get you all set up!

Setting Up Your AI Development Environment

1. Choose Your Operating System:

Before diving into AI development, you'll need to choose an operating system that suits your preferences and is compatible with AI tools and frameworks. The most common choices are Windows, macOS, or Linux. For beginners, Windows and macOS are user-friendly options. If you're already familiar with Linux, it's a great choice too.

2. Install Python:

Python stands as the programming language of choice for AI and machine learning applications, holding the position as the most extensively utilized in this field. It comes pre-installed on macOS and many Linux distributions, but you'll need to install it on Windows.

- Go to the official Python website (https://www.python.org/downloads/) and download the latest version suitable for your operating system.
- Run the installer, and during the installation, make sure to check the box that adds Python to your system's PATH. This will allow you to run Python from the command line easily.

3. Choose an Integrated Development Environment (IDE):

An IDE is a software application that provides comprehensive tools for coding, debugging, and running your programs. Some popular choices for Python development are:

- Visual Studio Code (VSCode): A lightweight, powerful, and customizable IDE developed by Microsoft.
- PyCharm: A full-featured IDE specifically designed for Python developers.

4. Install Required Libraries and Frameworks: AI development often requires specialized libraries and frameworks to build and train models efficiently. Some of the essential ones include:

- NumPy: For numerical computing and handling arrays and matrices.
- pandas: For data manipulation and analysis.
- TensorFlow or PyTorch: Popular deep learning frameworks.
- scikit-learn: For machine learning algorithms and tools.

5. Install Python and Libraries:

First, install Python from the official website. Then, use 'pip' (Python's package manager) to install essential libraries for AI: NumPy, Pandas, TensorFlow, and Scikit-learn. Open your command prompt or terminal and enter these commands:Copy code

```
pip install numpy pandas tensorflow scikit-learn
```

6. Virtual Environments (optional):

It's recommended to use virtual environments to keep your projects isolated. This prevents conflicts between package versions. Here's how to set it up:

- Install 'virtualenv' by running:

Copy code

```
pip install virtualenv
```

- Set up a virtual environment within your project folder:

Copy code

```
virtualenv venv
```

- Activate the virtual environment:
  - On Windows:
- Copy code

```
venv\Scripts\activate
```

  - On macOS and Linux:
- bash
- Copy code

```
source venv/bin/activate
```

Verify Your Environment: Open your chosen IDE (e.g., VSCode) and create a new Python file named "test.py." Copy and paste the following code into the file:

python

Copy code

```
import numpy as np import pandas as pd import
tensorflow as tf import sklearn
print("Congratulations! Your AI development
environment is set up successfully.")
```

7. Run the Test Code: Execute the "test.py" file in your IDE. You should see the message confirming that your environment is ready.

Introduction to Programming Languages for AI

Programming languages serve as the foundation for creating AI models, designing algorithms, and handling complex data processing tasks. As a beginner, it might seem overwhelming to choose the right programming language for AI, but fear not! This section will provide you with a clear overview of the most commonly used programming languages in AI and their key features.

Python: Python is undoubtedly one of the most popular and widely used programming languages for AI development. Its ease of use, clear readability, and adaptability render it a prime selection for newcomers. Python boasts an extensive collection of libraries and frameworks tailored explicitly for artificial intelligence and machine learning, including TensorFlow, PyTorch, and Scikit-learn.

These libraries enable you to build and train AI models efficiently, without getting bogged down in low-level details. Moreover, Python's robust community support ensures that you can find plenty of resources, tutorials, and code examples to aid your AI journey.

R: R is another programming language that finds extensive use in AI and statistical analysis. It provides powerful tools for data manipulation, visualization, and statistical modeling, making it a preferred choice for researchers and data scientists. While R might have a steeper learning curve compared to Python, it excels in certain statistical tasks and data analysis. If you are more inclined towards research-oriented AI applications or data-driven analysis, R could be a valuable addition to your AI toolkit.

Java: Java is a widely-used general-purpose programming language known for its portability and strong support for object-oriented programming. In the context of AI, Java might not be the most popular choice, but it is frequently used in developing AI applications for Android devices and enterprise-level systems. Some AI frameworks, like Deeplearning4j, cater to Java developers interested in building neural networks and deep learning models.

C++: C++ is a powerful and efficient programming language often used in performance-critical applications, including AI. While not the most beginner-friendly language, C++ offers high performance and control over memory management, making it suitable for computationally intensive AI tasks. C++ is often employed in developing AI applications for robotics, game development, and real-time systems.

Julia: Julia: Emerging as a recent programming language, Julia has garnered attention within the realms of AI and scientific computation. It boasts high-performance capabilities, with syntax resembling Python, making it easier for Python users to transition. Julia excels in numerical computing, which is crucial for AI tasks involving complex mathematical operations and simulations.

Lisp: Lisp, an older language, holds historical significance in the AI field. Its flexible nature and support for symbolic computing have made it popular in AI research and early AI projects. While not as prevalent today as Python or other modern languages, exploring Lisp can provide valuable insights into the history and evolution of AI development.

CHAPTER 5

BUILDING YOUR FIRST AI MODEL

Building an AI model involves couple of steps which include collecting and preprocessing data, choosing the right model for your task, training and evaluating it, and making improvements along the way. You don't need to be an expert in mathematics or programming to get started with AI; this guide will walk you through the process step-by-step. So, let's embark on this exciting journey together as we demystify AI and empower you to create your very own AI model!

Data Collection and Preprocessing

Data collection and preprocessing are fundamental steps in any AI project, and they play a crucial role in determining the success and accuracy of your AI model. Here's a practical overview of these processes, simplified for beginners:

1. Data Collection:
   - Identify the Purpose: Clearly define the purpose of your AI project and the specific problem you want to solve. This will help you determine what data you need to collect and what variables are relevant.
   - Select Data Sources: Decide where you will collect your data from. It could be from public datasets, APIs, web scraping, or even manual data entry.
   - Ensure Data Quality: Check the quality of your data to ensure it's accurate, consistent, and relevant. Deal with

missing values, outliers, and errors that could adversely affect your AI model.

- o Obtain the Right Format: Organize your data in a structured format suitable for analysis. Common formats include CSV, JSON, or databases like SQL.

- o Data Privacy and Legal Compliance: Be mindful of data privacy laws and regulations while collecting data. Ensure that you have the necessary permissions and consent to use the data for your AI project.

2. Data Preprocessing:

- o Data Cleaning: Clean the data by handling missing values, duplicates, and irrelevant information. This step is vital to improve the quality of your data and reduce noise in your AI model.

- Feature Selection: Choose the most relevant and informative features (variables) that contribute significantly to your AI model's performance. Removing irrelevant features can help reduce computational complexity.
- Feature Scaling: Normalize or standardize numerical features to bring them to a similar scale. This step prevents certain features from dominating the model due to their larger magnitude.
- Handling Categorical Data: Convert categorical variables into numerical representations, as most AI algorithms work with numerical data. Techniques like one-hot encoding or label encoding can be used for this purpose.
- Data Splitting: Divide your dataset into training, validation, and testing sets. The

training set is used to train the AI model, the validation set helps tune hyperparameters, and the testing set evaluates the final model's performance.

o Data Augmentation (Optional): For certain AI tasks like image recognition, you can augment your dataset by applying transformations like rotation, flipping, or scaling to increase its size and diversity.

Data collection and preprocessing are iterative processes. You may need to go back and forth between these steps to refine your data and improve your AI model's performance. Properly collected and preprocessed data sets the foundation for a successful AI project and enhances the accuracy and reliability of your model's predictions.

Choosing the Right AI Model for Your Task

When it comes to implementing artificial intelligence for a specific task, selecting the right AI model is crucial for achieving accurate and efficient results. For beginners, this process might seem daunting, but with a practical approach, you can simplify the decision-making process. Here's a step-by-step guide to help you choose the right AI model for your task:

- **Define Your Task**: Clearly articulate the problem you want the AI model to solve. Whether it's image recognition, natural language processing, recommendation systems, or any other task, having a well-defined problem statement is the first step.
- Research Existing Models: Look for pre-existing AI models that have been

developed and trained for tasks similar to yours. Libraries like TensorFlow and PyTorch offer a wide range of pre-trained models that you can leverage. Comprehend the strengths and constraints inherent in every model.

- Evaluate Model Performance Metrics: Determine the performance metrics that matter most for your task. It could be accuracy, precision, recall, F1 score, or other relevant metrics based on your specific needs. Consider the trade-offs between different metrics.

- Consider Model Complexity and Resource Requirements: Assess the complexity of the AI model and the resources (computational power, memory, etc.) needed to run it. For a beginner, starting with simpler models might be more manageable and less resource-intensive.

- Account for Data Availability and Quality: Take into account the availability and quality of your dataset. Some AI models require large amounts of labeled data for training, while others can perform well with limited data. Ensure that your data aligns with the model's requirements.

- Explore Transfer Learning:If you have limited data, consider using transfer learning. Transfer learning involves starting with a pre-trained model and fine-tuning it on your specific dataset. It can significantly speed up the training process and improve performance.

- Experiment and Compare: Don't hesitate to experiment with different AI models. Train and test multiple models to compare their performance on your task. This iterative process will help you gain insights into which model works best for your specific use case.

- Seek Community and Expert Advice: Join AI communities and forums to seek advice from experienced practitioners. Many experts are willing to help newcomers and can provide valuable insights on choosing the right model.

- Be Patient and Iterative: Remember that choosing the right AI model might involve some trial and error. Be patient and iterative in your approach. Take the time to understand the model's behavior and continuously refine your solution.

By following these practical steps, you can navigate the process of choosing the right AI model for their task more confidently and effectively. As you gain experience and knowledge, you'll become better equipped to make informed decisions about AI models for different applications.

Fine-Tuning and Improving Performance

Fine-tuning and improving the performance of an AI model are crucial steps in the development process.

Fine-tuning refers to the process of making small adjustments to an existing pre-trained model to adapt it to a specific task or dataset. This approach is particularly beneficial when you have limited data for your specific problem but can leverage a pre-trained model's knowledge from a related task. In this chapter, we will explore the concept of fine-tuning and demonstrate how it can be practically implemented even by beginners.

1. Understanding Fine-Tuning: We begin by explaining the concept of fine-tuning in detail, delving into why it is a valuable technique in AI development. By reusing the knowledge from pre-trained models, we can significantly reduce the computational resources required to train a model from scratch. We'll discuss the key components of fine-tuning, such as the base

model, the task-specific layers, and the learning rates.

2. Selecting the Right Pre-Trained Model: Choosing the appropriate pre-trained model for your task is essential. In this section, we'll explore popular pre-trained models like BERT, GPT-3, and ResNet, and guide readers on how to select the best fit for their specific AI project.

3. Data Preprocessing: Effective data preprocessing is crucial for successful fine-tuning. We'll walk readers through the steps of preparing their data for fine-tuning, including data cleaning, tokenization, and data augmentation techniques.

4. Fine-Tuning Neural Networks: This section will cover the step-by-step process of fine-tuning a pre-trained neural network. We'll provide practical code examples using popular AI libraries such as TensorFlow or PyTorch,

making it accessible for beginners to follow along.

5. Monitoring and Evaluating Performance: Fine-tuning may require a few iterations to achieve optimal results. Here, we'll discuss strategies for monitoring the model's performance during training, interpreting performance metrics, and deciding when to stop fine-tuning to prevent overfitting.

6. Hyperparameter Tuning: Fine-tuning often involves tuning hyperparameters to achieve the best performance. This section will guide readers through techniques for hyperparameter tuning, including grid search, random search, and Bayesian optimization.

7. Regularization and Dropout: To avoid overfitting during fine-tuning, regularization techniques like dropout can be employed. We'll

explain the intuition behind these methods and demonstrate how to implement them in practice.

8. Transfer Learning: Transfer learning is closely related to fine-tuning and has gained immense popularity in AI development. In this part, we'll explain the concept of transfer learning and how it can be utilized in tandem with fine-tuning to improve model performance further.

9. Troubleshooting Fine-Tuning: Fine-tuning can sometimes be challenging, especially for beginners. We'll address common issues that may arise during the process and provide practical tips to overcome them effectively.

10. Best Practices and Tips: To wrap up the chapter, we'll share some best practices, tips, and resources that will enable readers to fine-tune their AI models successfully and confidently. This will include learning resources, communities, and open-source repositories that

can be valuable assets for continuous learning and improvement.

CHAPTER 6

ETHICAL AND PRIVACY CONSIDERATIONS IN AI

Ethical concerns focus on fairness, transparency, and accountability in AI algorithms. Identifying and mitigating biases in the data used for training is essential to avoid discriminatory outcomes. Additionally, efforts should be made to make AI models more explainable to establish trust with users. On the privacy front, safeguarding personal data is of utmost importance. Developers must employ anonymization and encryption techniques to protect sensitive information. Clear guidelines for data usage, user consent, and transparent privacy policies are necessary to ensure user control and confidence.

In the ever-evolving landscape of AI technology, staying informed about emerging ethical frameworks and privacy regulations is vital. Emphasizing responsible AI development, where ethics and privacy are integral, paves the way for positive contributions to society while respecting individual rights. By nurturing a future where AI technologies coexist ethically with humanity, we can harness AI's potential for the greater good.

Bias and Fairness in AI Systems

When we talk about AI systems, it's essential to address the issue of bias and fairness. Just like humans, AI models can be influenced by bias, leading to unfair and discriminatory outcomes. Bias in AI refers to the systematic favoritism or discrimination towards certain groups or individuals based on attributes like race, gender, age, or socioeconomic status, which are present in the training data. This bias can result in harmful consequences, perpetuating stereotypes and reinforcing inequalities in society.

To understand how bias creeps into AI systems, let's consider an example. Imagine an AI system tasked with sorting job applications and deciding who gets called for an interview. If the training data used to develop this AI model predominantly consists of successful employees who were historically male, the model might learn to favor male candidates over female candidates. This is an example of gender bias, and it can lead to a lack of diversity in the workplace.

To promote fairness in AI, it's crucial to identify and mitigate bias in the data and the AI model. One approach is to carefully curate the training data, ensuring it represents a diverse and balanced set of examples across different demographic groups. This can help reduce the risk of bias being learned by the model. Additionally, data preprocessing techniques can be employed to remove or mitigate biased patterns from the data before training the AI model.

Another important step in ensuring fairness in AI is the regular evaluation and monitoring of the model's performance. AI developers must analyze the model's predictions for different subgroups and identify any discrepancies that may indicate bias. A fairness-aware evaluation involves measuring and comparing the model's accuracy, precision, and recall across various demographic groups to ensure equitable treatment.

Addressing bias and promoting fairness in AI is not only a technical challenge but also an ethical one. It is essential for AI developers and data scientists to be aware of their responsibility in creating AI systems that are fair and unbiased. Transparent documentation of the AI development process, including data sources, model architecture, and evaluation methodologies, can facilitate accountability and external scrutiny.

Fairness in AI is an ongoing process, as societal norms evolve, and new biases can emerge. Developers must be prepared to update and retrain AI models to address these changes and ensure the systems remain fair over time.

Bias and fairness are critical considerations in AI development. AI systems have the potential to impact people's lives significantly, and addressing bias is essential to avoid perpetuating discrimination and inequality. By being aware of the sources of bias, carefully curating training data, and regularly evaluating AI models for fairness, we can move towards building AI systems that treat all individuals fairly and promote inclusivity in the digital age.

Ensuring Data Privacy and Security

In the world of artificial intelligence, data is the lifeblood that fuels the growth and effectiveness of AI models. However, with the vast amounts of data being collected and processed, ensuring data privacy and security becomes a critical concern. As a beginner delving into the realm of AI, it's essential to understand the fundamental principles and best practices for safeguarding sensitive information.

Data privacy refers to the protection of personal or sensitive information from unauthorized access, use, or disclosure. To safeguard data privacy, individuals and organizations should adhere to certain principles. Firstly, data minimization should be followed, which means only collecting the necessary data for a specific AI task and avoiding the gathering of irrelevant or excessive information. Secondly, data anonymization and pseudonymization techniques should be employed to mask individual identities, ensuring data cannot be traced back to a specific person.

Implementing robust data security measures is equally crucial to protect data from breaches and cyber threats. Encryption plays a pivotal role in securing data both in transit and at rest. When data is encrypted, it becomes unreadable to unauthorized users, mitigating the risk of data interception during transmission or unauthorized access to stored data. Additionally, access control mechanisms should be established to restrict data access to authorized personnel only. This involves assigning different levels of access privileges based on roles and responsibilities within an organization.

For AI developers, it's vital to conduct regular security audits and vulnerability assessments to identify and address potential weaknesses in their AI systems. Employing cybersecurity experts can help ensure that AI applications are resilient to attacks and data breaches. Regular updates and patches to software and applications should also be performed to keep security defenses up to date, protecting against emerging threats.

Privacy by design is a principle that should be integrated into the AI development process. This involves considering data privacy and security from the outset of the project and throughout the entire development lifecycle. By proactively building privacy and security measures into AI systems, developers can create solutions that are privacy-conscious and less susceptible to vulnerabilities.

Another essential aspect of data privacy and security for AI is adherence to legal and regulatory requirements. Depending on the country or region, there may be specific data protection laws that mandate how personal data should be collected, processed, and stored. For example, the European Union's General Data Protection Regulation (GDPR) imposes strict guidelines on data handling practices, and non-compliance can lead to significant fines. Understanding and complying with such regulations is essential to avoid legal consequences and maintain the trust of users and customers.

Responsible AI Development and Deployment

Artificial Intelligence has the potential to revolutionize various industries and improve people's lives, but it also comes with significant responsibilities. Responsible AI development and deployment are essential to ensure that AI systems are fair, unbiased, secure, and aligned with ethical principles. The key aspects of responsible AI development include;

1. Fairness and Bias: One of the primary concerns in AI development is ensuring fairness and mitigating bias. AI algorithms learn from historical data, which may contain biases from the real world. If left unchecked, these biases can be perpetuated and lead to discriminatory outcomes. Responsible AI development involves identifying and addressing biases during the data collection and preprocessing stages. It's crucial to regularly audit AI models to detect and correct any unintended biases that might have emerged during training.

2. Data Privacy and Security: Protecting user data and ensuring data privacy is paramount in AI development. As AI systems often rely on vast amounts of user data, developers must implement robust security measures to safeguard this information from unauthorized access and breaches. Complying with data protection regulations and obtaining informed consent from users are critical steps in maintaining responsible AI deployment.

3. Transparency and Explainability: The "black-box" nature of some AI algorithms has raised concerns about the lack of transparency and explainability in decision-making. Responsible AI development involves using interpretable models whenever possible, allowing developers and users to understand how the system arrives at its conclusions. Providing explanations for AI-generated

decisions fosters trust and helps identify potential biases or errors.

4. Ethical Considerations: AI can impact individuals, communities, and society at large. Responsible AI development requires careful consideration of the ethical implications of AI systems. Developers should proactively assess the potential risks and benefits of their AI applications. This includes identifying scenarios where AI might be used for harmful purposes or exacerbate existing societal problems.

5. Human-Centric Design: AI should be designed with humans in mind, prioritizing user needs and preferences. Responsible AI development involves diverse perspectives and involves domain experts, ethicists, and affected stakeholders throughout the development process. Ensuring human-centric design minimizes the risk of deploying AI systems that

do not adequately address user requirements or values.

6. Continuous Monitoring and Evaluation: AI systems should be continuously monitored and evaluated after deployment. Responsible AI development includes regular audits to check for potential bias, performance degradation, or unintended consequences. Feedback loops should be established to gather user input and respond to emerging issues promptly.

7. Responsible Data Usage: Developers must be diligent in acquiring and using data responsibly. This includes using data only for the intended purposes, avoiding data exploitation, and adhering to data sharing agreements. Data should be managed with the utmost care to protect individual privacy and maintain trust with users.

8. Social Impact Assessment: Before deploying AI systems at scale, conducting a social impact assessment is crucial. Responsible AI development involves understanding how the AI application may affect different stakeholders, communities, and society as a whole. This assessment helps identify potential risks and ensures that AI is used to promote positive societal outcomes.

In conclusion, responsible AI development and deployment require a commitment to fairness, transparency, ethics, and user-centricity. It involves mitigating biases, protecting data privacy, and ensuring that AI serves as a force for good in society. As AI technology evolves, continuous learning and adaptability are essential for developers to stay up-to-date with best practices and ethical guidelines in the rapidly advancing field of artificial intelligence.

CHAPTER 7

FUTURE TRENDS AND APPLICATIONS OF AI

The future of AI is brimming with exciting possibilities, and this chapter delves into some of the most intriguing trends and applications that are expected to shape our lives in the coming years. One significant trend is the integration of AI in autonomous vehicles and transportation. Imagine a world where self-driving cars navigate busy streets, reducing accidents and optimizing traffic flow. Additionally, AI will continue to revolutionize robotics and automation, making tasks safer and more efficient across various industries.

Another compelling application lies in natural language processing and understanding. AI-driven virtual assistants and chatbots will become even more sophisticated, enabling seamless communication between humans and machines. These assistants will help us manage our daily tasks, answer questions, and provide personalized recommendations, making life more convenient and enjoyable.

AI is also set to play a pivotal role in addressing environmental challenges. From monitoring ecosystems to optimizing energy consumption, AI-powered solutions can contribute to sustainability efforts and foster a greener future.

However, as AI proliferates, it's crucial to address ethical and societal concerns. Ensuring fairness and mitigating bias in AI algorithms will be paramount to building a more equitable society. Additionally, discussions on data privacy and responsible AI development must remain at the forefront to safeguard individuals' rights and uphold ethical standards.

Overall, the future of AI holds immense promise and potential, but it requires responsible stewardship to harness its capabilities for the greater good. Embracing these trends and applications with awareness and a commitment to ethical practices will be vital as we move forward into an increasingly AI-driven world.

AI in Autonomous Vehicles and Transportation

AI has revolutionized the field of autonomous vehicles and transportation, paving the way for a future with safer, more efficient, and convenient transportation systems. In autonomous vehicles, AI plays a central role in making decisions and controlling the vehicle's movements without human intervention. Through a combination of advanced sensors, cameras, and radar systems, these vehicles continuously gather real-time data about their surroundings. AI algorithms process this data to recognize objects, detect obstacles, and predict potential hazards, enabling the vehicle to make informed decisions in real-time.

Machine learning algorithms are crucial in training autonomous vehicles to improve their decision-making capabilities over time. These algorithms learn from vast amounts of data collected during driving scenarios, allowing the vehicle to adapt to various road conditions, weather, and driving styles. Reinforcement learning, a subset of machine learning, is often used to fine-tune the vehicle's behavior based on feedback received during simulated or real-world driving experiences.

AI in transportation extends beyond autonomous cars. It also impacts traffic management systems, optimizing traffic flow by analyzing data from various sources, such as GPS devices and traffic cameras. Intelligent transportation systems leverage AI to monitor and manage traffic patterns, predict congestion, and recommend alternative routes to alleviate traffic jams. Additionally, AI-enabled predictive maintenance ensures efficient operations of public transport systems by identifying maintenance needs before they escalate into major issues, reducing downtime and costs.

Overall, AI's integration in autonomous vehicles and transportation holds the promise of safer roads, reduced traffic accidents, lower emissions, and enhanced mobility options for people worldwide.

AI in Robotics and Automation

AI's application in robotics and automation has revolutionized various industries, making repetitive tasks more efficient, reducing human error, and even enabling robots to perform complex actions independently. At the core of AI-powered robotics is the ability to sense, understand, and act upon the environment.

Sensors, cameras, and other data-capturing devices serve as robots' eyes and ears, allowing them to perceive their surroundings accurately. AI algorithms process this sensory data, enabling robots to identify objects, detect changes in the environment, and make decisions accordingly. These algorithms are often based on machine learning techniques like computer vision, natural language processing, and reinforcement learning.

In manufacturing, robots equipped with AI can handle assembly tasks with precision and speed. AI-driven robotic arms can quickly adapt to variations in product dimensions and perform quality checks, ensuring consistent output. In logistics and warehousing, AI-powered robots optimize inventory management and enhance order fulfillment by efficiently navigating through dynamic environments and autonomously picking and packing items.

Collaborative robots, or cobots, are designed to work safely alongside humans. AI algorithms play a key role in enabling cobots to recognize human gestures and intentions, facilitating seamless human-robot collaboration. This enhances productivity and safety, as robots can assist humans in physically demanding or hazardous tasks.

Outside the industrial domain, AI-driven robotic applications continue to advance, such as AI-powered drones used for surveillance, delivery, and search and rescue missions. Furthermore, AI is making strides in the field of healthcare, where robots can assist in surgeries, aid in patient care, and perform tasks in environments where human presence may be limited.

AI in Natural Language Processing and Understanding

Natural Language Processing (NLP) constitutes a captivating domain within artificial intelligence, focusing on the interplay between human language and computer systems. NLP enables machines to understand, interpret, and generate human language, opening up a wide range of applications that have become an integral part of our daily lives. One of the most familiar illustrations of AI-powered NLP is the virtual assistant found on our smartphones or smart speakers.

Consider Siri, the virtual assistant developed by Apple. When you ask Siri a question, it processes the spoken language and converts it into text, which it then analyzes and interprets using NLP algorithms. Siri then generates an appropriate response in a human-like manner, providing you with the answer you seek. This seamless communication between humans and machines is made possible by the power of NLP.

NLP is not only limited to virtual assistants; it is also extensively used in various text-based applications. For example, email filters that automatically sort spam emails from genuine ones employ NLP algorithms to analyze the content and context of messages. Similarly, language translation services like Google

Translate rely on NLP techniques to understand the source text and provide accurate translations.

AI in Environmental Sustainability

Artificial intelligence is proving to be a game-changer in the realm of environmental sustainability. The use of AI technologies to address environmental challenges has the potential to drive more efficient and effective solutions. One of the illustrative applications of AI in environmental sustainability is the optimization of energy consumption in smart buildings.

Imagine a smart building equipped with advanced sensors that monitor various environmental parameters like temperature, humidity, occupancy, and energy usage. AI algorithms analyze this real-time data to identify patterns and optimize the building's energy consumption. For instance, during periods of low occupancy, the AI system might adjust the heating, ventilation, and air conditioning (HVAC) settings to conserve energy while ensuring occupants' comfort. By using AI-driven energy optimization, buildings can significantly reduce their carbon footprint and contribute to environmental conservation.

AI also plays a vital role in monitoring and managing environmental resources. For instance, AI-powered drones can be used to survey and assess the health of forests, marine ecosystems, and wildlife populations. By analyzing data from aerial imagery, AI can help identify deforestation, track endangered species, and monitor changes in the natural environment over time. This information is invaluable for conservation efforts, allowing for timely intervention and sustainable management of natural resources.

Furthermore, AI is revolutionizing waste management practices. Smart waste management systems, enabled by AI, can predict fill-levels in waste bins and optimize waste collection routes. By minimizing unnecessary waste collections, cities can reduce fuel consumption and lower emissions from waste collection vehicles, contributing to cleaner air and a greener environment.

In conclusion, AI is proving to be a powerful ally in both NLP and environmental sustainability. In NLP, it enhances human-computer interaction, enabling virtual assistants and language-based applications to understand and respond to human language effectively. In environmental sustainability, AI-driven solutions are empowering us to conserve resources, optimize energy usage, and better manage our planet's precious ecosystems. As AI continues to advance, its positive impact on various aspects of our daily lives and the environment is only expected to grow.

CHAPTER 8

AI AND THE JOB MARKET

AI has significantly impacted the job market, reshaping the landscape across various industries. While AI brings forth automation and efficiency, it also raises concerns about job displacement. Repetitive and routine tasks are increasingly being handled by AI-powered systems, leading to the automation of certain job roles. However, AI has also created new opportunities and job roles that require expertise in AI development, implementation, and management. As the technology evolves, demand for AI specialists, data scientists, machine learning engineers, and AI ethicists has surged. To thrive in this AI-driven job market, individuals need to adapt by upskilling or reskilling to complement AI technologies. Companies are also focusing on human-AI collaboration, where AI augments human capabilities rather than replacing them entirely. Striking a balance between embracing AI's potential and nurturing human skills remains crucial for navigating the dynamic job market influenced by AI advancements.

The rise of artificial intelligence has had a profound impact on the job landscape across various industries. While AI brings about significant advancements and efficiency gains, it also disrupts traditional job roles, leading to a shift in the employment landscape. Jobs that involve repetitive and rule-based tasks are particularly vulnerable to automation. Tasks like data entry, manual data analysis, and certain manufacturing processes have increasingly been taken over by AI-powered systems, leading to job displacement for some workers.

However, it's important to note that AI doesn't only eliminate jobs but also creates new ones. As AI technology progresses, there is a growing demand for skilled professionals who can design, implement, and maintain AI systems. Jobs related to AI, such as data scientists, machine learning engineers, AI ethicists, and AI trainers, are becoming more prevalent as organizations seek to leverage AI for strategic decision-making and competitive advantage.

Preparing for an AI-Driven Future

As the influence of AI continues to expand, it becomes crucial for individuals to prepare for an AI-driven future. Embracing this technology can be empowering, but it requires a proactive approach to stay relevant in the job market. One of the key steps in preparing for an AI-driven future is upskilling and reskilling. As certain job roles become automated, individuals must acquire new skills that complement AI or focus on tasks that require human creativity, emotional intelligence, and critical thinking—qualities that machines still struggle to replicate.

Another essential aspect of preparation is to foster a learning mindset. AI technologies are continuously evolving, and staying updated with the latest trends and developments is essential for professionals to adapt and thrive in an AI-centric world. Online courses, workshops, and educational platforms can be valuable resources for gaining knowledge and expertise in AI-related fields.

Furthermore, individuals must understand the ethical implications of AI and participate in discussions about responsible AI development. Ethical considerations, such as bias in algorithms and data privacy, play a significant role in shaping the future of AI. Being informed and advocating for ethical AI practices will ensure that AI technologies are deployed in a fair and just manner.

Navigating AI Careers and Opportunities

For those interested in pursuing AI careers and opportunities, there are several entry points and paths to consider. The first step is to gain a basic understanding of AI concepts, which can be achieved through beginner-level online courses, books, or tutorials. Exploring the fundamentals of machine learning, data analysis, and AI programming languages is a great starting point .

Next, it's crucial to identify specific areas of interest within AI. AI encompasses a wide range of domains, including natural language processing, computer vision, robotics, and more. Newbies can find their niche by experimenting with different AI projects and exploring the various applications of AI in different industries.

Hands-on experience is invaluable in AI careers. Building AI models, working on real-world datasets, and participating in AI competitions can help individuals develop practical skills and a portfolio to showcase their expertise to potential employers.

Networking within the AI community is also essential for finding career opportunities. Attending AI conferences, meetups, and online forums allows newbies to connect with professionals in the field, gain insights, and discover potential job openings.

Finally, continuous learning is essential for success in AI careers. As AI technology evolves rapidly, staying up-to-date with the latest advancements and techniques is crucial to remain competitive and sought-after in the job market. Ongoing learning through online courses, workshops, and research papers will ensure that newbies can adapt to the dynamic AI landscape and make meaningful contributions to the field.

CHAPTER 9

OVERCOMING AI CHALLENGES

Overcoming AI challenges requires a comprehensive approach that addresses both technical and ethical aspects. On the technical front, developers and researchers must tackle issues related to data quality and availability, model selection, and training process optimization. They need to ensure that AI models are interpretable, reliable, and capable of handling real-world scenarios. Moreover, addressing biases and fairness concerns is crucial to building equitable AI systems. On the ethical front, transparency, accountability, and data privacy become paramount, as AI systems have the potential to impact individuals and society at large. Emphasizing a learning mindset, where failures are seen as opportunities for improvement, allows for continuous refinement and development of AI solutions. Collaboration between

AI experts, policymakers, and various stakeholders is essential to create responsible and beneficial AI technologies while minimizing potential risks and challenges.

Avoiding Common Traps in AI Implementation

Artificial Intelligence is a powerful technology with the potential to revolutionize various industries and aspects of our lives. However, developing and implementing AI systems comes with its own set of challenges and pitfalls. For beginners venturing into the world of AI, it's essential to be aware of these pitfalls to ensure successful and ethical AI projects. Here are some common AI pitfalls and how to avoid them:

1. Insufficient or Poor Quality Data: One of the most critical factors in AI development is the data used to

train the model. Inadequate data or data that is biased, incomplete, or of poor quality can lead to inaccurate and unreliable AI models. To avoid this pitfall, it's crucial to invest time and effort in collecting a diverse and representative dataset. Data cleaning and preprocessing are equally important to ensure that the data fed to the AI model is accurate and free from biases.

2. Overfitting and Underfitting: Overfitting occurs when an AI model performs exceptionally well on the training data but fails to generalize to new, unseen data. Conversely, underfitting occurs when the model is overly basic and fails to encompass the intricacies present in the data. To avoid these issues, it's essential to strike the right balance by using techniques like cross-validation and regularization during model training. These approaches help the model generalize well to new data without overfitting.

3. Lack of Domain Knowledge: AI algorithms can only be as good as the knowledge and insights provided to them. Developing AI systems without sufficient domain knowledge can lead to misguided results and decisions. To overcome this pitfall, collaborate with subject matter experts who can guide the AI development process and provide valuable insights. Domain expertise ensures that the AI system aligns with real-world requirements and produces meaningful outcomes.

4. Ignoring Ethical Considerations: AI can influence society in profound ways, and overlooking ethical considerations can lead to harmful consequences. Biases in data, discriminatory outcomes, or privacy violations are some of the ethical challenges AI developers face. To avoid this pitfall, integrate ethical principles from the outset of the AI project. Regularly

audit the AI system for biases and fairness and ensure data privacy and security measures are in place.

5. Failing to Monitor and Update AI Models: AI models are not static; they require ongoing monitoring and updates. Failing to monitor model performance and neglecting to update them with new data can lead to diminishing accuracy and relevance over time. Implementing a proper monitoring system and scheduling regular model updates can help maintain the effectiveness and reliability of AI systems.

6. Overlooking Interpretability and Explainability: In some domains, it's crucial to understand how AI models arrive at their decisions. Black-box AI models can be challenging to interpret, making it difficult to trust and rely on their outputs. Employing interpretable AI models or techniques that provide

explanations for their decisions can enhance transparency and user confidence.

7. Disregarding Human Expertise: AI should complement human expertise rather than replace it entirely. Overreliance on AI systems without considering human inputs and insights can lead to suboptimal outcomes. Remember that AI is a tool, and human expertise plays a critical role in defining problems, interpreting results, and making decisions based on AI outputs.

8. Unrealistic Expectations: AI is not a magical solution that can solve all problems effortlessly. Having unrealistic expectations about AI capabilities and timelines can lead to disappointment and project failure. Set achievable goals and milestones for AI projects, and be prepared to iterate and improve gradually.

AI development can be a rewarding journey if potential pitfalls are recognized and avoided. By addressing issues related to data, model performance, ethics, and human collaboration, beginners can pave the way for successful AI projects that contribute positively to the world. Embracing a learning mindset and seeking continuous improvement will also help developers adapt to the evolving landscape of AI and stay ahead in this exciting field.

Troubleshooting AI Models and Implementations

As you delve into the world of artificial intelligence, you'll inevitably encounter challenges when building and deploying AI models. Troubleshooting AI models and implementations is an essential skill to develop, as it allows you to identify and address issues that might arise during the development process. In this chapter, we'll explore some common problems you may encounter and provide simple, step-by-step approaches to resolve them.

- Data Quality and Preprocessing: One of the primary reasons for AI model issues lies in the data itself. Poor-quality or insufficient data can lead to inaccurate predictions and unreliable results. In this section, we'll discuss the significance of data preprocessing and how to handle missing values, outliers, and data imbalances. We'll also explore techniques to augment your dataset and ensure that your data is appropriately prepared for training.

- Model Selection and Hyperparameter Tuning: Choosing the right AI model architecture for your task is critical, and certain models may perform better than others depending on the problem you're trying to solve. We'll guide you through the process of evaluating different model options and introduce hyperparameter tuning to optimize your model's performance. By the end of this section, you'll be equipped with the knowledge to make informed decisions about model selection and fine-tuning.

- Overfitting and Underfitting: Overfitting and underfitting are common challenges in AI model training. Overfitting occurs when the model performs well on the training data but poorly on unseen data, while underfitting happens when the model fails to capture the underlying patterns in the data. We'll show you techniques like cross-validation and regularization to combat these issues and ensure your model generalizes well to new data.

- Computational Resources and Efficiency: AI models can be computationally demanding, especially when dealing with large datasets or complex architectures. Limited computational resources can lead to slow training times or even crashes. In this section, we'll discuss strategies to optimize your AI code and utilize hardware acceleration (e.g., GPUs) to speed up training and inference.

- Bias and Fairness: AI models are susceptible to inheriting biases present in the training data, which can lead to unfair or discriminatory outcomes. We'll explore methods to detect and mitigate bias in AI models to ensure ethical and equitable decision-making. Additionally, we'll emphasize the importance of diverse and inclusive datasets to reduce bias.

- Interpreting and Debugging AI Models: Understanding why an AI model made a specific prediction or classification can be challenging, especially with complex neural networks. We'll introduce techniques for model interpretation and visualization, enabling you to gain insights into how your model works and diagnose potential issues.

- Versioning and Deployment: Implementing AI models in real-world applications requires proper version control and deployment strategies. We'll cover best practices for managing model versions and ensuring smooth integration into production systems.

- Monitoring and Maintenance: AI models may require periodic updates and maintenance to stay relevant and effective. We'll provide guidance on monitoring model performance and data drift to spot potential issues and proactively maintain your AI solutions.

Embracing a Learning Mindset in AI

In the world of artificial intelligence, the most essential trait for both beginners and experts is a learning mindset. AI technologies are constantly evolving, and to stay relevant and make meaningful contributions, one must be open to continuous learning and improvement. Embracing a learning mindset in AI means adopting an attitude of curiosity, adaptability, and a willingness to explore new ideas and techniques.

1. Curiosity as the Driving Force: Curiosity is the cornerstone of a learning mindset. As a beginner, you should cultivate a natural curiosity about AI concepts, algorithms, and applications. Ask questions, seek answers, and don't be afraid to dive into complex topics. Curiosity leads to exploration, and in the

rapidly evolving field of AI, being curious will help you stay up-to-date with the latest advancements and breakthroughs.

2. Learning from Failures and Mistakes: AI development is often an iterative process, and failure is an integral part of it. Embracing a learning mindset means viewing failures and mistakes as opportunities to learn and grow. When an AI model doesn't perform as expected or encounters errors, don't get discouraged; instead, analyze the shortcomings, identify potential improvements, and iterate on your approach.

3. Continuous Education and Upskilling: AI is a multifaceted field, and there's always something new to learn. As a beginner in AI, invest time in continuous education and upskilling. Attend workshops, online courses, and read books and research papers to expand your knowledge.

Having a solid foundation and keeping abreast of the latest trends will empower you to tackle more complex AI challenges.

4. Embracing the Community: In the AI community, knowledge-sharing is abundant. Engage with fellow enthusiasts, join online forums, attend meetups, and participate in AI-related discussions. Embracing the community fosters a collaborative atmosphere where you can exchange ideas, learn from others' experiences, and gain insights that can propel your AI journey forward.

5. Practical Application and Projects: Theory is crucial, but hands-on experience is equally essential. Embracing a learning mindset in AI involves working on practical projects. Develop AI applications, experiment with different datasets, and engage in real-world problem-solving. Practical experience will

deepen your understanding of AI concepts and reinforce your learning.

6. Adapting to Change: The AI landscape is constantly changing. New algorithms emerge, tools evolve, and best practices shift. A learning mindset involves being adaptable and open to change. Be willing to explore new AI frameworks, learn novel techniques, and adapt your approach based on the latest industry trends.

7. Seeking Feedback and Collaboration: Feedback from peers and experts can provide valuable insights into your AI endeavors. Embracing a learning mindset means being open to receiving constructive feedback. Seek reviews of your AI models, collaborate with others, and be receptive to suggestions for improvement. Collaboration not only accelerates learning but

also exposes you to different perspectives and problem-solving approaches.

8. Ethical Considerations in AI: As AI technology advances, ethical concerns become increasingly important. Embracing a learning mindset involves being conscious of the ethical implications of AI development. Stay informed about AI ethics, privacy concerns, and fairness in AI applications. Strive to develop AI systems that align with ethical standards and contribute positively to society.

CHAPTER 10

THE FUTURE OF AI: POSSIBILITIES AND LIMITATIONS

This chapter aims to provide a balanced and accessible overview of the ever-evolving landscape of AI, empowering readers to embrace its possibilities while being mindful of the implications for society and humanity as a whole.

Speculating the Future of AI Technology

As we delve into the exciting world of artificial intelligence, it's natural to wonder what lies ahead for this rapidly evolving technology. While we can't predict the future with certainty, we can explore some potential directions that AI might take in the coming years. As AI continues to advance, its applications and impact are likely to expand significantly, transforming various aspects of our lives.

- AI in Everyday Devices: AI is expected to become increasingly integrated into everyday devices, making them smarter and more responsive to our needs. From smart home assistants like Alexa and Google Home to AI-powered smartphones, these devices will become even more intuitive and capable of understanding and anticipating our preferences. Imagine a future where your AI assistant knows when you wake up and automatically adjusts your thermostat, brews your coffee, and updates your calendar without needing explicit instructions.

- AI in Healthcare: AI's potential in revolutionizing healthcare is enormous. With advancements in medical imaging, AI algorithms can assist doctors in diagnosing diseases more accurately and detecting potential health issues at an early stage. AI-powered chatbots and virtual health assistants could become integral parts of patient care, providing personalized health advice and reminders for medication, helping to alleviate the burden on healthcare systems and improving patient outcomes.

- AI and Autonomous Vehicles: Self-driving cars have already made significant strides, and their development will continue to progress. AI technology will play a critical role in enhancing the safety and efficiency of autonomous vehicles, making transportation more reliable and reducing accidents caused by human error. The roads of the future might be filled with

AI-driven vehicles, potentially transforming the way we commute and travel.

- AI in Education: In the future, AI is likely to transform the education landscape. Personalized learning experiences powered by AI will adapt to each student's strengths and weaknesses, helping them grasp concepts more effectively. AI tutors and virtual classrooms might become common, extending educational opportunities to remote areas and learners of all ages. AI can also streamline administrative tasks, allowing teachers to focus more on teaching and student development.

As AI continues to evolve and integrate into various aspects of our lives, ethical considerations will become increasingly crucial. Ensuring that AI systems are fair, transparent, and unbiased will be vital in preventing discrimination and protecting individual rights. Striking a balance between the benefits of AI and potential risks will require ongoing vigilance and responsible decision-making by developers, policymakers, and society as a whole.

To quote noted computer scientist and AI researcher Andrew Ng, "AI is the new electricity. Just as electricity transformed almost everything 100 years ago, today I actually have a hard time thinking of an industry that I don't think AI will transform in the next several years."

Ethical and Societal Concerns in Advancing AI

As artificial intelligence continues to make progress and become more integrated into different aspects of our daily lives, it brings forth a range of ethical and societal issues. While AI holds immense promise for positive impact, it also raises significant questions concerning fairness, privacy, security, and human control. As a beginner in the world of AI, it is crucial to comprehend these concerns to ensure responsible development and use of AI technologies.

One of the most critical ethical problems with AI is bias. AI systems are only as good as the data they are trained on, and if that data carries biases, the AI model may perpetuate them, leading to unfair outcomes. For instance, facial recognition algorithms with biased training data could misidentify certain racial or ethnic groups, resulting in unjust consequences in areas like surveillance and law enforcement. Identifying and rectifying bias during AI development is essential to ensure fairness and impartial treatment for everyone.

AI's reliance on vast amounts of data also raises concerns about privacy and data security. AI systems may collect and process sensitive personal information, and if not adequately protected, this data could be at risk of breaches or misuse. Striking a balance between leveraging data for AI advancements and safeguarding individuals' privacy rights is of utmost importance.

As AI systems become more complex, their decision-making processes can become difficult to interpret, raising questions about accountability and trust. In fields like healthcare and finance, understanding how AI arrives at its conclusions is crucial for stakeholders. Ensuring transparency and explainability is essential to build user confidence and avoid the potential "black box" problem.

The growing integration of AI in various industries has raised concerns about potential job displacement. While AI can create new opportunities, it may also automate certain tasks, leading to workforce disruptions. Preparing for the future job market and ensuring a smooth transition for affected workers is a significant societal challenge.

Moreover, as AI applications expand into areas like autonomous vehicles and robots, concerns about safety become paramount. Ensuring AI-powered systems have robust fail-safes and can handle unexpected situations without endangering lives is crucial. The potential risks associated with fully autonomous decision-making raise important ethical questions.

In conclusion, while artificial intelligence presents tremendous potential for transforming various industries and enhancing our lives, we must address the ethical and societal concerns accompanying its progress. By promoting transparency, fairness, privacy protection, and safety in AI development and implementation, we can ensure that AI becomes a force for positive change, benefiting society as a whole.

Embracing AI for Positive Change

Over the past few years, Artificial Intelligence (AI) has seamlessly integrated into our everyday existence, transforming diverse sectors and presenting ingenious answers to intricate challenges. However, there have been concerns about its potential negative impact on society and the job market. To address these concerns and harness the full potential of AI, it is essential to focus on embracing AI for positive change. This means utilizing AI technologies to create a more inclusive, sustainable, and equitable world. As AI professionals emphasize, the key lies in understanding the transformative power of AI and steering its development towards the betterment of humanity.

Elon Musk, CEO of Tesla and SpaceX, once said, "AI is a fundamental risk to the existence of human civilization." While his statement reflects the potential risks associated with AI, it also underscores the importance of channeling AI's capabilities towards positive outcomes. This sentiment is shared by many AI experts who advocate for ethical AI development. By establishing robust frameworks for data privacy, bias mitigation, and accountability, AI can be designed to respect human values and rights.

Dr. Fei-Fei Li, a renowned AI researcher and co-director of the Stanford Institute for Human-Centered Artificial Intelligence (HAI), believes that "AI should be an amplifier of human values, not a replacement."his philosophy highlights the idea that AI ought to enhance human capabilities, not supplant them. For example, in the healthcare industry, AI-powered medical diagnostics can assist doctors in making more accurate and timely decisions, ultimately improving patient outcomes. By empowering human potential through AI, we can create a symbiotic relationship that drives positive change in various fields.

One of the most promising areas where AI can drive positive change is environmental sustainability. Dr. Andrew Ng, a leading AI researcher, emphasizes that "AI can help save the environment at scale." AI technologies, such as predictive modeling and data analytics, can aid in monitoring ecosystems, analyzing climate patterns, and optimizing resource utilization. By harnessing AI's potential in sustainability efforts, we can work towards mitigating the impacts of climate change and creating a greener future for generations to come.

Another aspect of embracing AI for positive change involves addressing socio-economic challenges. As AI continues to reshape industries and the job market, there is a need to ensure a just transition. Kai-Fu Lee, the CEO of Sinovation Ventures, believes that "AI will have a disruptive effect on many people's jobs, but it will also create many opportunities." By investing in reskilling and upskilling programs, societies can equip their workforce with the necessary skills to thrive in an AI-driven world. Furthermore, AI can enable new job opportunities and unlock economic growth in previously untapped domains.

AI can also be a powerful tool for promoting inclusivity and accessibility. Sundar Pichai, CEO of Google, expresses that "AI has the potential to improve the lives of billions of people." Through AI-powered assistive technologies, individuals with disabilities can experience greater independence and participate more fully in society. Additionally, AI language translation services break down language barriers, fostering cross-cultural understanding and cooperation.

Embracing AI for positive change requires collaboration between policymakers, industry leaders, researchers, and the general public. Open dialogue and multidisciplinary cooperation are essential to ensure that AI technologies align with societal goals and values. As Dr. Timnit Gebru, a former AI Ethics Researcher at Google, puts it, "We need diverse voices to create AI that benefits all of humanity." Inclusivity in AI development ensures that the technology reflects the needs and perspectives of a diverse global population.

In conclusion, AI has immense potential to drive positive change across various domains, from healthcare and sustainability to socio-economic empowerment and inclusivity. As AI professionals advocate, the focus should be on harnessing AI's capabilities responsibly, ethically, and inclusively. By prioritizing human values and collaborating towards a shared vision of AI for the greater good, we can create a future where AI serves as a catalyst for positive transformation, benefiting individuals and society as a whole. Embracing AI for positive change can pave the way for a brighter and more equitable world, making AI a powerful force for good in the 21st century.

GLOSSARY OF KEY AI TERMS

- Artificial Intelligence (AI): AI involves simulating human-like intelligence in machines to perform tasks such as problem-solving and decision-making, mirroring human capabilities.

- Machine Learning: Machine Learning is a subset of AI where computers learn from data, improve performance over time without explicit programming, and make predictions based on data patterns.

- Deep Learning: Deep Learning, a specialized Machine Learning form, trains multi-layered artificial neural networks for complex tasks like image recognition and language processing.

- Neural Networks: Neural Networks are computational models inspired by the brain's structure, processing information to recognize patterns and make decisions.

- Supervised Learning: In Supervised Learning, models learn from labeled data, mapping inputs to correct outputs for tasks like prediction.

- Unsupervised Learning: Unsupervised Learning trains on unlabeled data, discovering patterns and relationships without explicit guidance.

- Reinforcement Learning: Reinforcement Learning teaches AI models through rewards and punishments, learning by interacting with an environment.

- Natural Language Processing (NLP): NLP enables machines to understand and generate human language, crucial for virtual assistants and chatbots.

- Data Preprocessing: Data Preprocessing readies data for analysis by cleaning, transforming, and formatting it correctly.

- Bias in AI: Bias in AI leads to unfair outcomes due to biased data or algorithms, highlighting the need for unbiased AI systems.

- Training Data: Training Data is used to teach AI models, containing input examples and corresponding expected outputs.

- Overfitting: Overfitting happens when an AI model performs well on training data but poorly on new data, impacting generalization.

- Algorithm: An Algorithm guides AI systems step by step to solve specific problems or tasks.

- Feature Engineering: Feature Engineering selects and transforms data features to enhance AI model performance.

- Predictive Analytics: Predictive Analytics forecasts future outcomes using historical data and AI models.

- Computer Vision: Computer Vision enables machines to interpret visual data from images or videos, used in object detection and more.

- Robotics: Robotics combines AI, machine learning, and mechanics to create autonomous robots.

- Chatbot: A Chatbot is an AI conversational agent used for support, information retrieval, and virtual assistance.

- Sentiment Analysis: Sentiment Analysis uses AI to identify emotional tones in text, like social media posts or reviews.

- Autonomous Systems: Autonomous Systems are AI-driven machines like self-driving cars or drones that perform tasks independently.

- Data Science: Data Science extracts insights from data, using statistics and machine learning techniques.

- Cloud Computing: Cloud Computing provides internet-based computing services, aiding AI development without local hardware.

- Hyperparameters: Hyperparameters are pre-training settings affecting AI model learning.

- Convolutional Neural Network (CNN): A CNN specializes in image and video processing, using convolutional layers for feature extraction.

- Natural Language Generation (NLG): NLG creates human-like text or speech using AI, for chatbots and content creation.

- Internet of Things (IoT): IoT links physical objects via sensors and software, with AI processing their data.

- Autonomous Vehicles: Autonomous Vehicles use AI to drive and navigate without human control.

- Expert Systems: Expert Systems simulate human expertise using rules and knowledge bases for decision-making.

- Natural Language Understanding (NLU): AI skill enabling machines to comprehend and respond to human language accurately.

- Image Recognition: AI's power to categorize and identify objects, people, or patterns in images.

- Big Data: Vast and intricate data requiring AI for analysis and insights extraction.

- Cloud AI Services: Pre-built AI tools by cloud providers, simplifying integration for developers.

- AI Ethics: Addressing moral and societal implications of AI, encompassing fairness, bias, and transparency.
- Training Data: Information for teaching AI, including input samples and correct output labels.
- Model: AI's trained algorithmic representation for predictions and analysis of new data.
- Deep Learning: Complex pattern recognition using interconnected neural networks.
- Neural Network: Computational model mimicking the human brain's structure and function.
- Artificial Neural Network (ANN): Specialized neural network for AI and machine learning tasks.
- Inference: Using trained AI models to predict or decide on unseen data.

- Underfitting: Poor model performance due to simplicity or inadequate training.
- Feature: Measurable property extracted from raw data for AI analysis.
- Preprocessing: Data cleaning, transformation, and normalization before AI training.
- Transfer Learning: Using pre-trained models as a starting point for new tasks.
- Reinforcement Learning: AI learning through environment interaction and feedback.
- Ethics in AI: Addressing ethical concerns and societal impacts of AI technology.
- AI Agent: Entity perceiving its environment and taking actions to achieve goals.